The Equilibrium Line

The Equilibrium Line
David Wilson

smith|doorstop

Published 2019 by
Smith|Doorstop books
The Poetry Business
Campo House
54 Campo Lane
Sheffield S1 2EG
www.poetrybusiness.co.uk

ISBN 978-1-912196-74-6

British Library Cataloguing-in-Publication Data.
A catalogue record for this book is available from the
British Library.

Designed & Typeset by Utter
Printed and bound by CPI Group (UK) Ltd, Croydon, CR0 4YY
Cover image: Climbers on the Bluemlisalp traverse above
Kandersteg, Switzerland, by kind permission of Mike Pescod,
Abacus

Smith|Doorstop is a member of Inpress,
www.inpressbooks.co.uk. Distributed by NBN International,
Airport Business Centre, 10 Thornbury Road Plymouth PL 6 7PP.

The Poetry Business receives financial support from
Arts Council England

Contents

Part Three

Part Four

For my family and my friends on the hill, with gratitude

Part One

Lines of Ascent

To W H Murray, Mountaineering in Scotland

Your book was a tent I slept in each night,
your mountains so fiercely imagined
my London life felt like exile.

I climbed with you up moonlit snow
in glare so bright we wore dark glasses.
Our blue shadows danced beside us.

I watched you work with a slater's pick
to carve holds in walls of green ice,
only halfway as darkness welled up.

From your prisoner-of-war camp you wrote
that retreat under fire to El Alamein
held less suspense than Observatory Ridge.

I studied the guides, unfolded the maps,
but you put the hills at the end of my street,
and every winter your snow still arrives.

Bivouac at Harrison's Rocks

Leaves turn from green to grey.
On the breeze, a scent of hops.
A star appears. A bat.

Beyond silver birches
a train sounds its two-tone horn,
slows for a bend, disappears.

We're fifteen years old
with apple pies, cans of Sprite,
and dreams of the Eigerwand.

Above our ledge a sandstone roof,
below us the drop. Not far
but far enough.

The Slab

This is for Spring ... that you may remember.
— Les Murray

The slab tilted up for five hundred feet or more.
Slate-grey, with veins of white quartz,
it lay in an amphitheatre of rock, split by gullies
that oozed and dripped. All afternoon I'd sat
waiting by a green lake at the slab's foot
for the last climbers to coil their ropes and leave
so I might take it on unseen,
protagonist in my own drama
or making a fool of myself alone.

I tightened my second-hand kletterschue,
slung borrowed rope around my neck,
lifted my arms and touched the rock,
still warm from late sun but now in shadow.
The mountains held their breath.
It was time, time to make my move
and be gone, time to reach for the small flake
I'd studied for hours, to curl fingers round it,
place my boot on the quartz edge and climb,
the slab flowing beneath me, offering its holds,
unrolling in an almost-blur of moving up till
I was higher than the roof of our house,
the science block at school, the church spire,
moving up and up, the lake below shrinking
to a single calm eye. It was time

as it would be time that night to walk
to the edge of heavy-scented pines
beyond all artificial light,
and give thanks to mountains
who'd been generous that day;
time to look up at stars fiercer and brighter
than I'd known, pressing down,
breathing in, breathing out.

Feeding the Crow
In Memoriam Dave Knowles

Hughes' *Crow* explained the world,
your father's early stroke,
America in Iraq.

You translated words into rock,
gritstone cracks which hung in space,
hand-jams that bit our flesh.

You wanted steep, hard, cold,
a printer's landscape of black and white,
and so to Nevis in February,

an unclimbed buttress in a storm.
Crow is loving this, you said.
Your dark eyes shone.

High in a vertical ice-choked groove
your crampons slipped and scraped.
I had no belay worth the name,

prayed to a kinder, weaker god
that we might get out of this alive.
Crow grinned, and flew his black flag.

Summer with Yeats

Our climb's in a zawn
of Bosigran granite
above turquoise sea.

We're near the top
of the graded list,
scene of many falls, but

I know the sequence,
do not stop to
think this time;

each hold finds
me, shapes my
moves. Now. And

now. And now, as
through cold fingers
glittering summer runs.

Gritstone Solo, Sudden Rain

What was here an hour ago has gone;
people, lark-song, sunlit purple,
a shout that would be heard.

Now the climb demands you be
the self you always sought.
Calm legs that want to tremble,

dry each shoe against your jeans,
then commit to one small edge,
your life balanced on its tip.

On top, high, look down the long slab.
It's three hundred million years old.
That's how close you came to time.

The Minutes

As I sit to write up the Minutes,
the *White Spider* is hiding under a file
and I can see the tower of Centrepoint
pale against blue sky. I begin to dream

of the Eigerwand, lead the Difficult Crack
in style, jam, bridge, pull over a roof,
keeping my rhythm, barely bothering
to clip in-situ pegs, worn wooden wedges,

traverse the Hinterstoisser, every step history
and homage, three thousand feet below us,
the shadow of the face and beyond that,
sunlit pastures, the sound of bells drifting

up along with sirens from Oxford Street.
Under the press of the Minutes,
we cut to the start of the Ramp.
A storm hits; hail, lightning, falling rocks;

chimneys become cascades, slush pours
down sleeves. No choice now but to bivouac,
show *White Spider* fortitude. The temperature drops
as the sky clears. We're racked with shivers.

Dawn. My hands grip the edges of my desk.
I lead up icy cracks, swing and test each axe,
pull up an overhanging bulge; we pass relics
of past attempts, a twisted piton, blood-stained rock,

but still we move up, to reach the Brittle Crack
as winter dusk descends on Tottenham Court Road.
Unstoppable, we gain the Traverse of the Gods,
the Minutes still unwritten.

Alpine Bivouac

A luxury ledge as darkness quickens.
We tie ourselves in, backs to the wall,
light the stove for a first brew,
twist a Mars Bar in half.
A plane cruises past, each window lit.
We belt out 'Bread of Heaven'.
This is the hour of plenty.

Lightning behind the Aiguilles,
each flash an electric skeleton.
Clouds ghost across Orion,
putting out its stars one by one.
Thoughts turn to ugly descent,
the hanging glacier, mist and snow.
This is the night watch.

Shivery half-sleep through dreams
of work. You nudge me awake.
From east to west the sky is clear.
Nothing trickles, creaks, whirrs.
The skin of ice on our water pan
captures the fire of the rising sun.
This is our moment.

The Drop

Trapped, I watch my fingers,
numbed by cold, uncurl.
My dead weight drops.

You're twisted sideways,
hold me as rope burns your wrists.
I fall in a place I promised not to,

the easy pitch, no runners on,
a so-so belay and exposed.
I fall for weeks.

It wasn't the biggest fall I'd take
but nonetheless a rehearsal,
for looking up at where I'd been,
and down to where a heart could break.

Bwlch y Moch, Tremadog

I cross the causeway into the past,
arrive early, Eric's Caffi not yet open,
the barn still here where we lived for a summer,
fresh hay once a week, the walls a gym for wet days.
Was the adder in the sink a myth, I wonder
as I swing over a gate and into a field
from where the silver-grey crag looks a facade,
so long it is since I climbed here.

But names come back, each releasing another,
Kestrel Crack, One Step in the Clouds, Merlin Direct,
then up a grade to *The Plum*, where Yes fought No
for fifty metres. And on, to *First Slip, The Grasper,*
Nimbus, the language of rock becoming familiar
until we were almost native speakers;
and *Vector*, where sketchy teenage selves
found for a while force and direction.

We went further afield when we had lifts,
to the Cromlech with its crozzly pockets,
to Dinas Mot, Cyrn Las and Cloggy,
to just-discovered Castell Cwydm
and Anglesey's *Dream of White Horses*,
and on north to the Cuillin ridge,
the Ben in winter to purify the soul,
and south, east and west to continents.

But this was home, nothing grand but a friendly
terrace of a crag, mild, with good protection,
and this barn filled with plans and fun,
where I say my friends' names.
Without you it would have been nothing.
I could stay here forever in early summer
between Vector Buttress and the sea.
And I will.

A Place for Bearings

Hold

Remembering my sister

During the time we were a family
we went behind the scenes at London Zoo.
The keeper prodded a rattlesnake
so we might hear it seethe.
A straggly-haired orang-utang
hung an arm around you.
You fed it grapes. And smiled.

But mainly I remember the alligator,
how only you would hold it.
You turned your hands palms up,
let the pale belly rest there,
looked down at its armoured skin.
And stood, said nothing, stared ahead,
as if knowing you'd hold it all your life.

Falling

The Continental Cafe, Leicester Square.
Pitta breads, falafels, coffees.
I'd been buying a present in Foyles,
you were alone on your north face.
Nothing I said made any difference.
You were falling and I could not hold you.

At the tube station we hugged each other.
You leaned your head briefly against me,
filled with the thoughts that gave you trouble.
Through blurring eyes I watched you
descend into the Underground.
You were falling and I did not hold you.

Yr Wydffa, November

I need my old familiar hill
fierce with wind and rain;
push hard past Lyn Lyddaw,

the ruins of Britannia mine.
Crags and hillsides run white;
rain finds every opening,

dissolves the membrane
that lies between two worlds.
So I have come to this grief

as if you'd waited here for me,
half-way up the Miners' Track,
standing under slate rain.

The Problem

As if it were an answer, I drive north
past Pulpit Rock and Rannoch Moor
to rendezvous below the Buchaille.
March. The coldest day for ten years.

Ice chokes our water bottles.
A frozen flapjack chips a tooth.
I tie the figure-of-eight wrong,
stare down at the dumb knot.

Brittle with cold, we swing and kick,
curse the hot aches, move up
to belay high in the gully
below its chockstone pitch.

Forced onto the chasm's left wall,
I hook and teeter on smears of ice,
nearly barn-door, reach higher,
place my bet, fully exposed,

until I'm clear and over the worst,
to gasp and tremble and roar
as my heart emerges from the cave
where it's crouched all winter.

Ben Nevis, Still Life

All day we climb inside a white room,
white mist for its walls, ceiling, floor,
our breath pluming white into air
dappled with lightly falling snow.

Pitches enter, play their part and leave –
a rock step, a snow traverse, a groove.
Flickering in and out of existence,
a black buttress, a ghostly face.

Below our feet there's no exposure,
a fall would be into white mist.
It curtains us inside each moment,
this clink of hexes, a crampon squeak.

On top it's calm and featureless white,
as if the mountain's emptied of thought.
A place for bearings, on which we'll descend,
opening and closing countless white doors.

A Stone

Was it too much to want a life
where she might have her own dog,
and once in a while climb Ingleborough
on a winter's day when the Irish Sea
runs silver along the western coast;

and rest at the top in a dry-stone fold,
protected from the east wind's bitterness,
then choose a stone the colour of sea
to skim across the summit plateau,
her dog leaping after it and searching

amid the thousand for that one
holding the scent of her hand,
then racing back to drop it at her feet
and look at her with bright eyes,
perhaps one green, the other brown?

As she flung the stone again
there'd be nothing but her tensed arm,
the universal blue of sky
and local green of valleys,
and her dog flying back to her alone.

Bluebird Day 1

Its buttresses feathered with white rime,
the Ben soars through dazzling light.
Dave says we've earned this from our storms.

Our climb's a gully between rock walls
narrowing to a roof of blue sky,
the ice plastic, steep and fat.

I remember to breathe, keep an A shape,
feet apart, hips in, arching back
to swing and flick each axe in turn

and rise with unexpected ease as if
I've air sacs in my bones and this day
has conjured a lighter, stronger self.

Back down, we unclip crampons,
flex fingers that were claws,
peel and share an orange.
And the day comes home.

The End of Winter

Water-drops like tadpoles
wriggle behind skins of ice.
Snow slopes run to green.

I came here for one last climb
but the gully that I dreamed of
is turning back to shattered rock.

Melt is everywhere.
Too many layers,
my thoughts drip with sweat.

Going back, I watch a mountain hare,
its winter-white coat perfect
for a landscape no longer there.

Part Two

Beta

Ed calls up, 'What's the problem?'
'It's a cheeky little number,' I say,
'probably sandbagged, never its grade'.

I could take a screamer, even deck out,
was far too lax about placing pro.
Our warm-up climb is taking me down.

Stuck on a ledge, I know Ed's thinking
his grandma could push a pram up this.
He won't want to climb with me again,

so I make a move towards the crux.
Legs start to Elvis.
'Trust the rubber!' Ed shouts,

'Cut loose! Spin that shit!!'
But I'm back at my ledge,
not sending the climb

or smashing it,
while a voice whispers,
'This is how your life could pass.'

Mediocrity

From Latin: medius – middle, ocris – rugged mountain

You caught up with me again at Stoney Middleton,
stuck half-way up a lower grade climb.
We'd met off and on over the years,
in chemistry lessons, karate, electric guitar.
Now you were at my shoulder as I slunk back to my car
too ashamed to stop for a brew at Lovers Leap.
You tried to console me by saying how on easier routes
we'd meet more interesting, generous people,
like that group from Bordeaux who partied late
and next day staggered up the Aiguille du Tour
in a carnival of songs, laughter and broken crampons.
You said the greatest invention of the Twentieth Century,
apart from sticky-soled rubber rock shoes,
was Klein's concept of 'good enough'.

On Thursday night we argued outside the Testosterone Arms.
You urged me past, told me not to drink in a place
where climbers deal in grades and the only currency is hard.
And how I was never high enough up the hierarchy
to chalk my name for darts or catch the eye
of Nancy from Huddersfield. I was torn,
but you said I should accept things and enjoy myself,
as we'd soon be meeting more.

God's Own Rock

I torque myself into the crack,
push, pull, chicken-wing, thrutch,
determined to land the first punch.

A crucial fist-jam pierces flesh.
My gritstone heart does not flinch.
I knew this was a Whillans route.

How did he climb up into my skin,
that youth too pumped to grip his pint,
full of the gunpowder smell of the crack,

desperate for more off-width life,
his knuckles flaps, a denim knee dark
where God's Own Rock blooded him?

Pen-y-Ghent

Grass gives way to slippery limestone,
the trusty friction of blocky grit.
Walking's rhythm untangles my day.
I think best on my feet.

Where would I be without you
taken-for-granted home hill?
I bring my rain, sun, mist,
you welcome me whatever.

And if I wonder what I am made of
you show me a raven surfing the breeze,
dusk gathering in the folds of hills,
a light coming on in a distant house.

Indoor Weather

Remember the dark moor,
dawn slogs to high crags,
the disappointment of rain.

Remember those times you were gripped,
the fall when half your hexes ripped out,
bruises appearing like storm clouds.

Come in from your grit and granite
to this hall of coloured holds
with calm, conditioned air.

The problems here are well-designed:
blue, black, white, red – various
selves, most of them satisfied.

While cold rain steams the windows
let music play within the walls,
let mats cushion every fall.

T S Eliot at the Climbing Wall

Tattooed between Jo's shoulder blades
a face I know peers out:
two vertical lines dividing the brows,
hair slicked back, sharp parting,
spectacles with round retro frames.

Around Eliot's head
his words made flesh –
Do I dare
Disturb the universe?
Yes, Jo does, happily.

She climbs up on crimps and slopers.
Supple muscles tense and release,
animating Eliot's face.
How optimistic this makes me feel.
How many ways there are to live!

Hers and His

After the glare of glaciers,
the changing room is dark.
Soon the air will chill.

I haul off my T-shirt,
rummage in a plastic crate,
pull out my thermal vest.

It's tight under the arms.
Sweat and sun-cream stains
smell less familiar.

'That's mine,' you say. We smile,
peel off tops and swap,
already changing.

Stanage Edge, October

Summer's returned for one day only,
blue sky, no wind, mist in the valleys,
bracken turning the colour of fox fur,
the Edge's gritstone silver in the sun.
Rock warm to touch. But holds won't sweat.

You check your harness, knots and rack,
lay away, step high and up again to poise
off-balance, wriggle a cam into place,
then smear a slab, heels low, until
a crack grips your outstretched hand.

We linger on the edge. Smoke rises
straight up from the chimney at Hope.
It's not a day to hurl ourselves against
but for dancing with, to feel alive
on *Black Slab, Inverted V, Goliath's Groove.*

And it will light the long edge in our minds,
where name after name spells a life,
Flying Buttress and *Left Unconquerable,*
holds we could trust to always be there,
winds which threw every word away.

A Run Round Raven Crag

So many trees thrown down by winter storms.
Their torn and tangled roots are shocked.
Saplings have snapped, taken new forms –
a clash of antlers, a praying mantis.

My track blocked by logging trucks,
I climb a bank where ferns unfurl
and fungi work on hollowed stumps.
Between moss-covered rocks a fairy glen.

Chainsaws release pine-breaths. And I
run on, through leaf litter and slime,
from down to up, and up to down,
a work in progress, a work in regress.

To the Mont Blanc Range

You were the cable car ride to the top
of the year, the slight shudder as it docked.

You were the ramp onto an evening ferry,
an hour's sleep in a stubbly field;

the drive south to *Tequila Sunrise*,
a first beer in the Bar Nationale.

You were Rebuffat's *Hundred Finest Routes*,
a line to die for on a card;

big boots, sweating hands, granite cracks,
'a moment of weakness at altitude'.

You were Snell's Field in midday sun,
exhaustion stuck to a karrimat,

and a crate of cauliflowers nicked
from a stack outside *Intermarche*.

You were festering days in damp tents
and lightning striking where we'd been.

You were the one tent that stayed empty;
and a voice we needed to listen to.

You were midnight starts wild with stars.
You were headlamp beams. You were spots of time.

Le Lac Blanc

How good not to be bound for the Triolet this year,
its steep, hard-to-read, trapezoid north face.
How much better to cruise these well-worn paths
that zig-zag up through sweet-smelling pines
to clearings with benches and multi-lingual signs.

No serac barriers here, no dark ice to question.
No need to bivouac on gravel by the moraine,
fret about the *meteo*, set alarms for midnight,
then shed my thin bag of sleep, and, by torchlight,
try to work out what's under the glacier's page.

How much better to lounge on a sunny terrace
outside the Refuge du Lac Blanc, with people
who do not know or want to know the names –
the *Niche* on the Dru where lightning hissed,
The Shroud and *Walker* on the Grandes Jorasses.

Why bother with this fading language when instead
I can drink coffee by a pale glacial lake and watch
these mirrored monuments of rock and ice tremble
in a cross-wind. No white void. No need to stand
in a sling clipped to an ice-screw and watch it bend.

Tonight in the hut I'll break bread with new friends,
drink late, then retire to my silk liner with no need
to write by torchlight of how I bridged a groove
coated in rime and punched my ice-axe through
a cornice to be dazzled by light from the other side.

Falling Upwards

The old man sits on a bench, breathless,
harness squeezing his paunch.
Limps back to the wall,
dips his hands in chalk,
curls fingers around an edge,
levers a foot onto a hold.

Then pulls himself up
for a moment of lightness
when one move opens into the next,
and all of him is lifted,
his test results, his dodgy hip,
the nape of his neck she liked to kiss.

Almscliff Boulders

An all-night labour, forceps at dawn.
And then there are three of us.
Back home I play 'Isn't She Lovely'
over and over, sing, dance, cry some more.
It feels natural then to go to Almscliff,
thrusting out its gritstone chest
from slopes above the Wharfe Valley,
where barley fields are pale gold.
I close my eyes and rest against a slab
in warmth so perfect it's hard to know
where my body starts and ends.
New forces have been released today.
I bring the news of my daughter's birth,
and Almscliff gifts me a problem
I've tried and failed at all my life.

Darker Blue Depths

Red, Yellow, Glas

Owen sees rests as white space;
says nothing; wants no exchange,

is looking to find his form,
The Corner followed by *Vember*,

tells me off for taking a stance
his guidebook doesn't sanction.

I want to end with *Bow-Shaped Slab*.
Too soft, he says, proposing *Bloody*.

He thinks in lines, standards, rules,
horizontals, verticals, right angles,

like mountains conceived by Mondrian,
my yellow useful to show his red

strong against it. Somewhere inside him
the blue so hard to translate from Welsh.*

* 'glas' – blue and green, sky and grass

Fjarski

Out of the blue, she tells him
about fjarski, the Icelandic word
not so much for distance itself,
as difficulty in judging distances;

how perspective blues horizons;
or the way hills appear to retreat
as dry air grows moist. He notes
the word half-rhymes with fiasco

and walks out into the blue hour
when dog is hard to tell from wolf.
Later, he returns, to search her eyes.
He can't unlearn this new word.

Snow Bridges

His daughter's twelve, her face pale.
The pink specs are new, he thinks.
His first mistake's to sit opposite.
A half for him, for her a coke.

He glances down at Saturday's paper.
Looks up. She looks away.
He asks the names of her friends,
what sports she likes at school,

says he's off to the Alps soon,
would love to go with her one day;
is thinking of changing his car,
not sure if the old one will make it.

After silence, she meets his eyes.
If you could choose any colour ...?
'Probably dark blue,' he mutters.
Mine would be silver, Dad.

He shifts his chair and leans in.
They're still roped up, thank God.
How deep these crevasses,
how delicate their snow bridges.

Alpine Partner

I was thinking of glaciers as metaphors,
you knew the car park's exit code.
And you'd practised techniques
for rescue from a crevasse,

to dig a T slot, bury your ice-axe,
attach our *micro-traxion* gadget,
then fix the rope as a Z-haul
across the sweating surface, so that inch

by inch you heaved me up when I fell,
up from that cold place – its white walls,
fins of green ice, pale blue caves,
darker blue depths beyond saying.

Part Three

Mallory

Preserved by cryogenic cold
he's made a statue of himself.
I shouldn't rubberneck but do.

His arms wide and half-raised as if
for victory, or to break his fall;
his back bare, slabbed with muscle,

the skin alabaster-white; right leg
corkscrewed, but otherwise he's perfect,
as if Death had been re-enchanted

after Flanders. He's still attached
to the rope as we are to him:
old hero with your *manly daring*

I do not want to see you explained
but leave you high on the North East Ridge.
How could they bear to turn you over?

Everest

Once it was Chomolungma,
Mother Goddess of the Earth,
a face whose veil rarely lifted,
its whiteness the White Whale's.

Now it's like Elvis near the end,
a giant in a soiled jumpsuit,
blank, useful for percentages,
a sheet from which the music's fled.

Expedition, 1972

After days spent high on the climb
she carries down sanitary pads
to burn on a base camp fire.
The circle of men falls silent.

Here in the Karakoram –
Black Gravel in Turkic –
she walks off their maps
into whiteness

The Climber
In Memoriam Wanda Rutkiewicz 1943–1992

1961

Wanda tip-toes up a sunlit slab,
wraps her hands round a spike; hesitates,
then reaches for the heart of a chimney-crack,
back-and-foots and jams against its sides.

She's climbing solo. Friends are shocked.
But she's finding all the holds she needs.
Tonight there will be vodka and songs,
Stalin jokes, a dry cave for sleep.

Churches, smokestacks, lamentations
fall away below her into white mist,
Five Year Plans, queues for food, the broken
walls and people in her twice-betrayed house.

She finds a pebble at the top, smooth,
round, containing nothing but itself.
From today she'll build from summits,
snow, ice, a hundred floors of air.

1992

Crouched in a niche carved from snow,
Wanda faces down the Kanchenjunga night,
alone, at twenty-seven thousand feet,
no water, sleeping-bag or stove.

She should have followed her torch-beam
down the breadcrumb trail of ice-axe marks
to fixed ropes, food, warmth. But then
to where? And what end? With who?

Instead, the long Polish night continues.
The blood-red, ash-grey courage
of Winged Hussars, W-hour, Gdansk
keeps alive her eight thousand metres plan.

Dawn breaks at minus twenty, silhouettes
Everest, white against grey-blue.
Frost-nipped fingers paw at frozen boots.
Breath comes hard, air burns her throat.

But still she climbs, her steps inches now.
And should we imagine her happy?
The girl who ran a ruined home at five,
the woman who spurned the token slots

on men's expeditions, early Solidarność.
Sheltered by seracs, embalmed in ice,
for eulogy the summit wind,
Wanda will never be found.

In Praise of Sleet

Artist of the passing moment,
it floats, falls, dissolves;
isn't deep; doesn't accumulate,
impose a blank year-zero page.
Wouldn't dream of making a scene.

It has no grand plan for transfiguration,
won't stop retreats from Moscow
or you reaching Tesco.
Doesn't want you to lie down and be an angel;
leaves Michael Furey's grave untouched.

Doesn't have fifty names for itself;
no need to fret if it fails to arrive,
to think of fractured Arctic shelves
and polar bears trapped on floes
like double mattresses cast adrift.

It won't haunt you with a melting story
about how you should have left more tracks
in December in Minnesota, or called across
a glistening slope to Marie, 'hold on tight'.
It slips away while Brueghel mixes paint.

Generations

What did she think of those climbers
whose routes lie on sun-warmed rock,

on waves of yellow sandstone
and basalt columns like organ pipes,

or above swells of aquamarine
in Madagascar or Majorca?

They climb in red and yellow lycra,
falls protected by bomb-proof bolts,

chalk absorbs their fingers' sweat,
rubber shoes stick to holds.

They have no father's war to fight
or test their courage against,

they have no wall within themselves
which they must risk their lives to cross.

Kashmir Lines

Kalashnikovs stooked against the snow
offer a clue to the Line of Control,

then a blown-off foot in a khaki sock,
deep-frozen into a mountain boot.

A glacier snakes between rock ridges,
its medial moraine a zig-zag stripe.

The ice is littered with pools of melt
from pipes laid in to fuel the troops.

Between two tents they've strung a line
on which their kit will never dry.

Via Ferrata Delle Trincee, Dolomites

Inside the mountain's tunnelled body
even with torches we can't see far,
stumble up steps hacked out of rock,
take false turns that end in openings
for snipers, mortars, machine gun nests.

We're in the dark about who fought who
and where the front line froze for years,
don't know of White Friday avalanches
or generals waiting for '99'ers'
to reach eighteen, supply fresh blood.

We grope our way into sunlight,
down rocks once covered in crosses.
A howitzer stands on level ground,
with nothing now to protect except
marmots and sky-blue gentians.

The Cave

An afternoon storm, hail, lightning,
thunderclaps like blows to the head.
We're crossing a moonscape of rock,
already dusk, everything drenched.

Half-way up a barren slope
the dark oval of a cave,
tall, deep, dry-floored.
Nearby, a miracle of brushwood.

We build a fire, steam sleeping bags dry;
nothing on the climb will compare.
Now, held by the cave's walls,
we can tell our scary stories;

the melting Rwenzori ice cap,
shrinking the Nile in its bed;
the hyena that bit off someone's face
while they slept outside near here.

Warming Air
From Rabelais

The glacier groans as it contracts,
its equilibrium line lost.
Words long-frozen start to thaw,
some sharp, some blunt, some bloody;
and pale blue and green words
that melt as we try to pick them up.

Above Arolla, Swiss Alps
After SB Banks

That night we stay in a high hut, mingle with climbers
and hikers from Seoul, Seattle, Tel Aviv; sit outside and
watch snow peaks turn from gold to pink to cold grey;
retreat indoors to benches and tables.

'If the climate is changing', one guy says, 'I'm bloody
glad it's getting warmer!' There's a pause. Facts melt as I
try to retrieve them.

Then we ladle out soup, push and pull plates, share
bread and stories from the day, no one wanting to ruin
the atmosphere.

Bonatti's Hands

For CAN

I had perhaps testified by my exploits to
the constant possibility of going further ...
–Walter Bonatti

Knuckles swollen, tendons cords,
his old hands rest on a wooden table,
fingers scored but the tips smooth
that once were cut and frost-bitten.

Gone at a stroke, the South West Pillar,
his masterpiece of hand and eye,
collapsed into night, thousands of tons
where he climbed past K2.

Conquistador of the Useless perhaps.
Yet, thick-veined where dreams pumped,
his hands reach out to touch us;
this problem that seems impossible

worked out, pitch by pitch –
its red slabs and pendulums,
fissures capped by overhangs,
its blank walls, and fingers of rock

lassoed with a bolas of knots,
the rope climbed hand over hand –
and a line found that we might follow
till what was in front lies behind.

Part Four

After Work, Almscliff Crag

Held in place
by drystone walls
green fields bring
my mind to order.

Among scattered boulders
my favourite slab,
mirror-smooth,
a balance problem.

The first move up
gathers me in,
the next becomes
my only fact.

Crampons

I thought I'd given you away.
But opening a jiffy bag in the attic,
there you are: same black spikes
and anti-ball plates, same bindings,
not a fumble with straps, rings, buckles,
but the slip of a boot into a bail,
the pull and snap of a clip.

Tell me again about being single-minded,
about couloirs bulging with fat blue ice
and dawn arriving high in the Alps;
how a slope exists at a perfect angle
where it all might kick in again,
on névé so pure your front-points hold
with just the lightest tap of my toes.

In the Balance

You pause beneath a boss of ice
above a thousand feet of space.
The picks of your axes barely bite:
it's bullet hard, black with rock dust.
You've run out forty feet of rope,
placed only an ice-screw and screamer.
You've dreamed of this route for half your life.
Your calves burn. You can't wait long.

Decision time. Weigh the following:
an abseil retreat to blankets, pasta, beer;
the taste in your mouth if you bottle out;
November at work without a fix;
a glimpse of where the pitch might ease;
her face at a window, Dad come home,
and you not knowing where you've been
or how to get back from it.

The Rucksack

Your key turned in the lock,
rucksack shrugged off.
Then, family not yet back,
a mug of tea, bath running,
water whispering in pipes.
The end of every climb is home.

The rucksack bides its time.
Inside its zipped-up lid
the compass still finds north.
Soon there'll be a pull in the air,
a day filled with slanting sun
and wind that stirs the leaves.

Avalanche, Ben Nevis

How softly we climbed that winter,
touching the snow as if it were skin
on the slope that led to the routes,

knowing they were somewhere beneath us,
partners who left their tent at dawn,
her in her blue jacket, him his new boots.

It could as easily have been us,
lost beneath an unreadable surface
as layers of old and new compressed.

On the Misty Summit of the Ben

After hacking our last pitch to pieces,
through helmet, hood and balaclava
I dream of hearing birds, then see them –
white with black-tipped wings,
migrants whose south is our north,

perched on rocks, circling, landing,
up here, like us, for no good reason,
and up here well, at home in snow,
their touch so light they leave no marks,
transform this whiteness into song.

Equilibrium

Climbing dissolves me in colour,
orange-red blur of heart effort,
blue precision of balancing up.
Ice becomes my picture plane,

the blank surface I pattern with marks.
Our line curves up from the drop below
through to the top of our frozen world.
At every point my placements hold.

We rest at the summit. Landscape stills.
Beyond white hills the sun sets
where islands, sky and sea-lochs merge:
I am here again, I am here after all.

We go back the way we came,
share stories in the listening dusk.
Above Stob Coire's silhouette
two stars balance a crescent moon.

Falling into Place

This V-groove with an overlap
where, stretched, I search icy cracks,
and feel my ice-axe pick lock tight

against the journey through the dark
how much does this crux weigh?
And this descent through blind cloud,

crampons scritching over windslab
as blasts of spindrift pepper skin,
against the level weeks that follow,
how much does it all weigh

or this spot in time when mist clears
and we see at length the Black Cuillin
written in a continuous stroke
across the pale north-western sky?

Sunday Morning Pass, Dolomites

A biker flows through hairpin bends,
left and right, smooth as an eel.
Forests give way to sunlit pastures.
We're singing along to our playlist,
a spire of silver rock behind us,
holding yesterday's beautiful climb.
We might go to Slovenia today,
or not.

At the top of the pass, hikers step from buses,
cyclists raise their arms in triumph,
and parapentistes queue for cable cars,
backpacks holding their coloured wings.
No one is here to sow division
or mine the land or pick the blue gentians
that only grow where the air is pure.
We know how thin the topsoil is.

Bivouac with Stonefall

Pressed hard against my bones
the heart presents its evidence;
pressure, pain, chaotic pulse,
thumps echoing off walls.
The years ricochet past.

To be with love a little longer,
track it across dry glaciers
to its old green meadows.
But the mountain wears out.
The skull shows beneath the skin.
Stonefall in the night, stonefall in my heart.

Bluebird Day 2

Mid-April at the climbing wall.
A good place to pass an hour
on a damp Saturday morning.

I start with espresso at Café Indulge,
turn through yesterday's Times
searching for the Mind Games section

but finding myself at the Register
where Malcolm died peacefully
and Jeannie suddenly passed away.

At the wall Sajid gives me a hug,
Jo shows us a one-armed yoga stand.
Then we laugh and clap and offer tips

competing over the problems
the route-setter's just put up.
Jo's T-shirt proclaims Utopia.

Erasure
from 'The Eastern Approach' by George Mallory

When all is said about Chomolungma
                                I come back to the valley
the broad pastures
            where cattle grazed   the little stream

saxifrages, gentians and primulas
                        and a soft, familiar blueness in the air

but

                        a night of early moons
            under our feet the granular atoms of fresh fallen snow

                            rising from the bright mists
Mount Everest above us

            steadfast like Keats's star

In the Beginning
In Memoriam Chris Yeoman

The clag right down, only one torch,
we fumble our way up the track,
bent under the weight of a tent
with a lead ventilation pipe.
Surplus, you said, from Everest.
We pitch it blind on stony ground.

Enough then to be under canvas,
to feel the guy-ropes keep us tethered
as wind shook the roof and walls;
to watch the blue flame of the stove
and listen to rain like wild applause,
the darkness outside perfect.

Down

We've had our fill of edge and jagged and carrying
weight. How good to be back on flat ground,
an Alpine village, tables under the stars,
pizza stringing up to our mouths,
glasses of red leading us south.

Who knows what starts us laughing, perhaps
Paddy's joke about three dogs at the vet's
or Hilary quoting her dad's secret diary
but it all follows in one mass,
our lives, whatever possessed us.

Eyes stream, we gulp for air,
our laughter tonight a funnel
through which everything passes,
everything that's happened,
everything that will.

Praise Song

Praise for the luminous dome of Mont Blanc
rising above our dark valley,
how such light pulls us up;

praise for the power of names,
the Central Pillar of Freney,
Sentinel Rouge, Innominata;

and for the single bivouac light
on the black mass of Argentière Wall,
its tiny flame in a mineral world;

praise for fresh snow at the glacier's head;
may it gather in every depression,
fill the dry collecting ground;

praise for being here with my daughter,
who touches the back of my neck,
says each line came from looking up.

Acknowledgements

Versions of some of these poems have appeared before: in poetry magazines including *The North*, *Poetry News*, *Rialto* and *Poetry Salzburg*; and in climbing magazines including *Alpinist* online (USA), *Climb*, *Scottish Mountaineer* and *BASE*. A few others were prize-winners in competitions and first appeared on their web-sites.

Some poems, for example, 'Lines of Ascent', are about how climbing stories live in my imagination, rather than being strictly accurate.

My heartfelt thanks go, firstly, to Ann and Peter Sansom, their team at Smith|Doorstop and everyone in the classes of '12 and '14; and to Jon Barton, Jim Caruth, Ian Duhig, Jane McKie, Helen Mort, David Pickford and Stuart Pickford.

Notes

The Equilibrium Line

The altitude on an alpine glacier where snow gained (accumulation) is equal to ice lost (ablation).

The Slab

Inspired by Les Murray's 'Spring Hail'.

Feeding the Crow

The title nods to Al Alvarez's book *Feeding the Rat*, and the last line echoes Ted Hughes' 'Crow Blacker Than Ever'. 'Nevis' is Ben Nevis, colloquially known as 'The Ben'.

The Minutes

After John Ashbery, 'The Instruction Manual'. *The White Spider* is a history of climbing on the North Face of the Eiger (Eigerwand), written by Heinrich Harrer, one of the team who made the first ascent in 1938. It's a book that has inspired generations of climbers.

A Stone

'Universal blue' and 'local green' are from 'The Middleness of the Road' by Robert Frost.

God's Own Rock

Don Whillans was famous for bold and strenuous routes. 'God's Own Rock' is gritstone, especially in Yorkshire and the Peak District. My gritstone poems owe a debt to the writing of Jim Perrin.

To the Mont Blanc Range

'a moment of weakness at altitude' is from Gaston Rebuffat, legendary French climber and guide. 'Spots of time' is from Wordsworth's 'The Prelude'.

Le Lac Blanc

After Billy Collins' 'Consolation'

Red, Yellow, Glas

The words in italics are names of climbs on Clogywn D'Arddu in North Wales.

Fjarski

'The blue hour' refers to a time at dusk, and the French saying, 'L'heure entre chien et loupe'. This poem was inspired by the Icelandic artist and poet Ásta Fanney Sigurðardóttir

Mallory

In 1999, an expedition found and searched Mallory's body for clues about whether he and Irvine reached the summit in 1924.

The Climber

Wanda Rutkiewicz had a deeply difficult childhood, her family torn apart by the Nazi occupation of Poland and then tragedies during the Soviet era. A great mountaineer, her ambition was to climb all fourteen eight thousand metre peaks. See, for example, *Caravan of Dreams* by Gertrude Reinisch and *Freedom Climbers* by Bernadette McDonald.

In Praise of Sleet

Michael Furey is Gretta Conroy's first love who died young in *The Dead* by James Joyce. Sleet is used in the UK sense of a mix of rain and snow that melts as it meets the ground.

Warming Air

From *Gargantua and Pantagruel*, by Francois Rabelais, Chapter 56.

Dellee Trincee Via Ferrata, Dolomites

'White Friday' refers to avalanches which killed over two thousand soldiers and dozens of civilians.

Walter Bonatti's Hands

Walter Bonatti's brilliant solo ascent of the South West Pillar of the Petit Dru was climbed in the bitter aftermath of an expedition to K2 where Bonatti was falsely accused of sabotaging two other climbers' summit attempt, an accusation he was cleared of after many years had passed. The quote is from Walter Bonatti, *Mountains of My Life*. *Conquistadors of the Useless* is the autobiography of the great French climber Lionel Terray.

CAN is Community Action Nepal, which supports the mountain people of Nepal by community-directed projects. Much of its work was destroyed in the earthquake of 2015. CAN's aim then was to re-build 'better and more'. All author proceeds from this book will be donated to CAN.

Climbing terms and slang

Anti-ball plates: sheets of plastic fitted to crampons to stop snow building up, which can turn crampons into clogs!

Barn-door: a swing sideways, e.g. when one ice-axe pulls out.

Beta: information about how to climb a particular route, e.g. the hardest moves or the protection needed (from Beta Max).

Cam: a device fitted into cracks to protect a lead climber. It has spring-loaded metal cams which grip the rock.

Crux: the hardest move or moves on a climb.

Deck out: hit the ground.

Hex: hexagonal metal wedges of various sizes, fitted into cracks to protect a lead climber.

Névé: snow which has been through freeze-thaw cycles resulting in a firm surface that's good for ice-axe and crampons.

Micro-traxion gadget: a pulley that locks the rope, capturing what's gained as a climber is hauled from a crevasse.

Pro: see Runner below

Rack: the collection of climbing equipment used to protect a climb.

Runner (running belay): clipping the rope through a karabiner attached to a sling. The sling might be round a spike of rock or attached to a cam or hex placed in a crack, or to a bolt. Runners reduce the length of a fall by the leader. Placing runners is typically called pro (protection) or gear.

Sand-bagged: a route that is harder than its stated grade, as if one is weighted down.

Screamer: a sling which has stitches designed to rip and thereby absorb the energy of a fall. Typically used with doubtful ice-screws. Screamer also refers to a long and scary fall.

Sending it: completing a route or boulder problem.